When Mum Died

The pictures tell the story of the death of a parent in a simple but moving way. Adolescents and adults with learning difficulties (mental handicap) will find the pictures are meaningful with or without the text. The book will help to inform readers about the simple facts of death and about feelings of grief. For bereaved readers the story may parallel their own experience. Parents, friends or professionals will be able to help them share their own story of loss, and guide them to new hope in their own futures — just as the story ends on an optimistic note. The story begins and ends in the family photograph album, and readers are encouraged to turn to their own album later.

When Mum Died

Sheila Hollins
Lester Sireling
Illustrated by Elizabeth Webb

St George's Hospital Medical School
LONDON
in association with
Silent Books
CAMBRIDGE

First Published in Great Britain 1989
by St George's Hospital Medical School, Cranmer Terrace, Tooting,
London SW17 0RE
in association with Silent Books, Swavesey, Cambridge CB4 5RA

© Text and illustration copyright Sheila Hollins and Lester Sireling 1989

No part of this book may be reproduced in any form, or by any
means without the prior permission in writing from the publisher

ISBN 1 85183 020 0

Typeset by Goodfellow & Egan, Cambridge

Printed and bound in Great Britain by
HGA Printing Company Ltd. Brentford Middlesex

To our parents and our children.

With thanks to the following people whose interest and encouragement has made this book possible: Nigel Hollins, Joan Bicknell, Enid Fairhead, Freda Macey and Sue Redshaw.

This is a picture of Stephen with his family. The story tells us what happened when his Mum died.

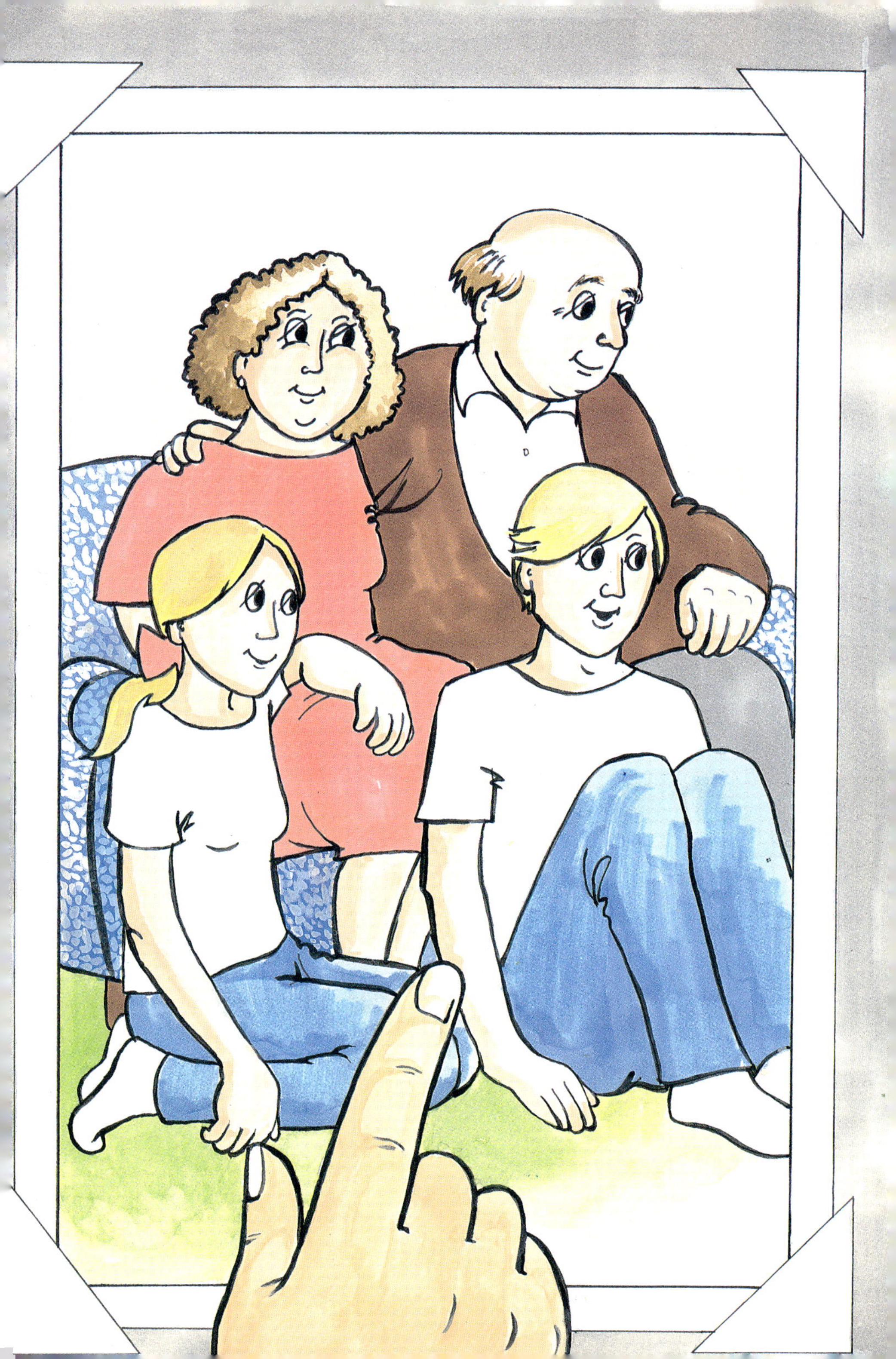

One day Mum had a pain.

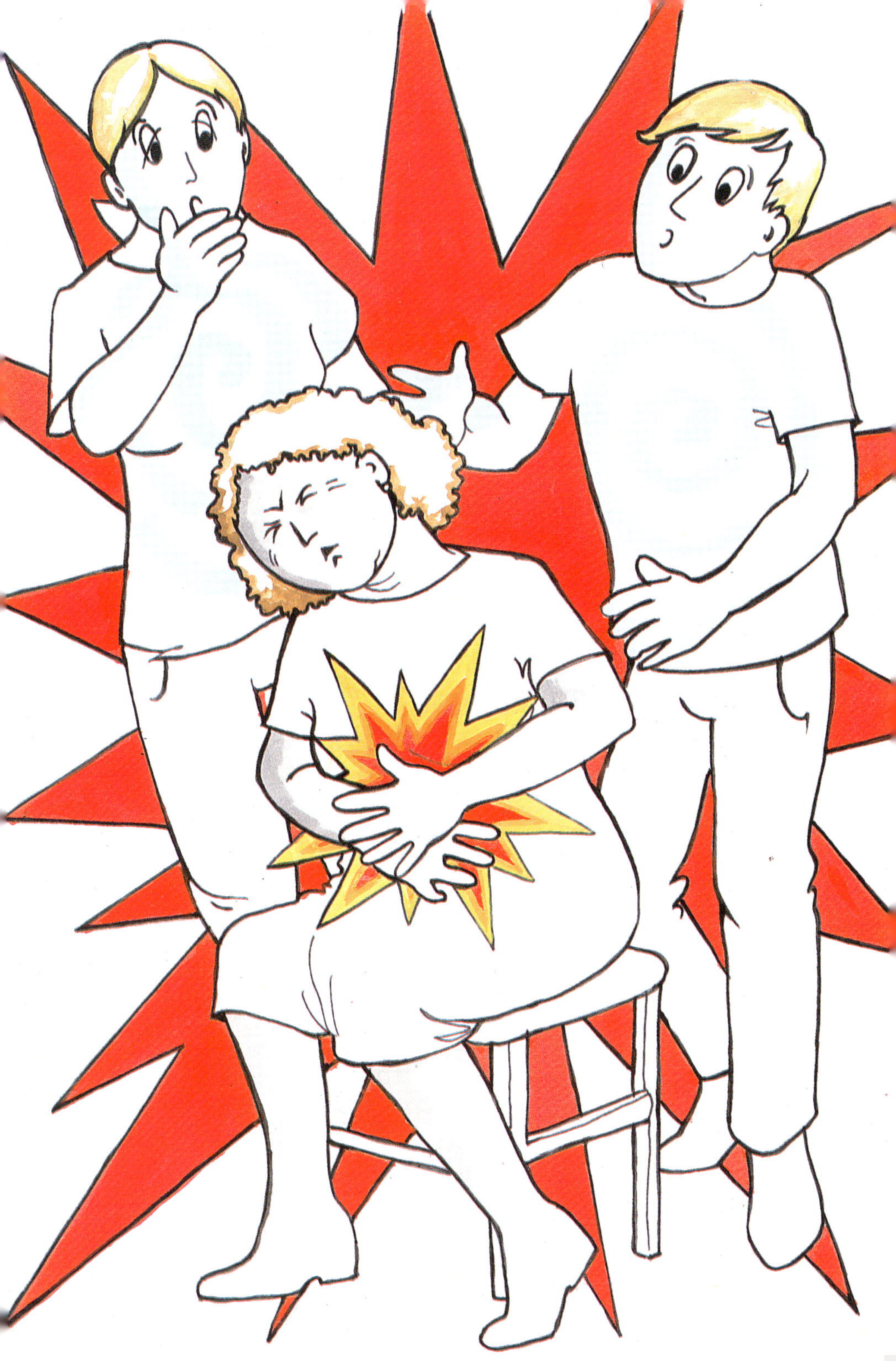

Dad phoned 999 for an ambulance.

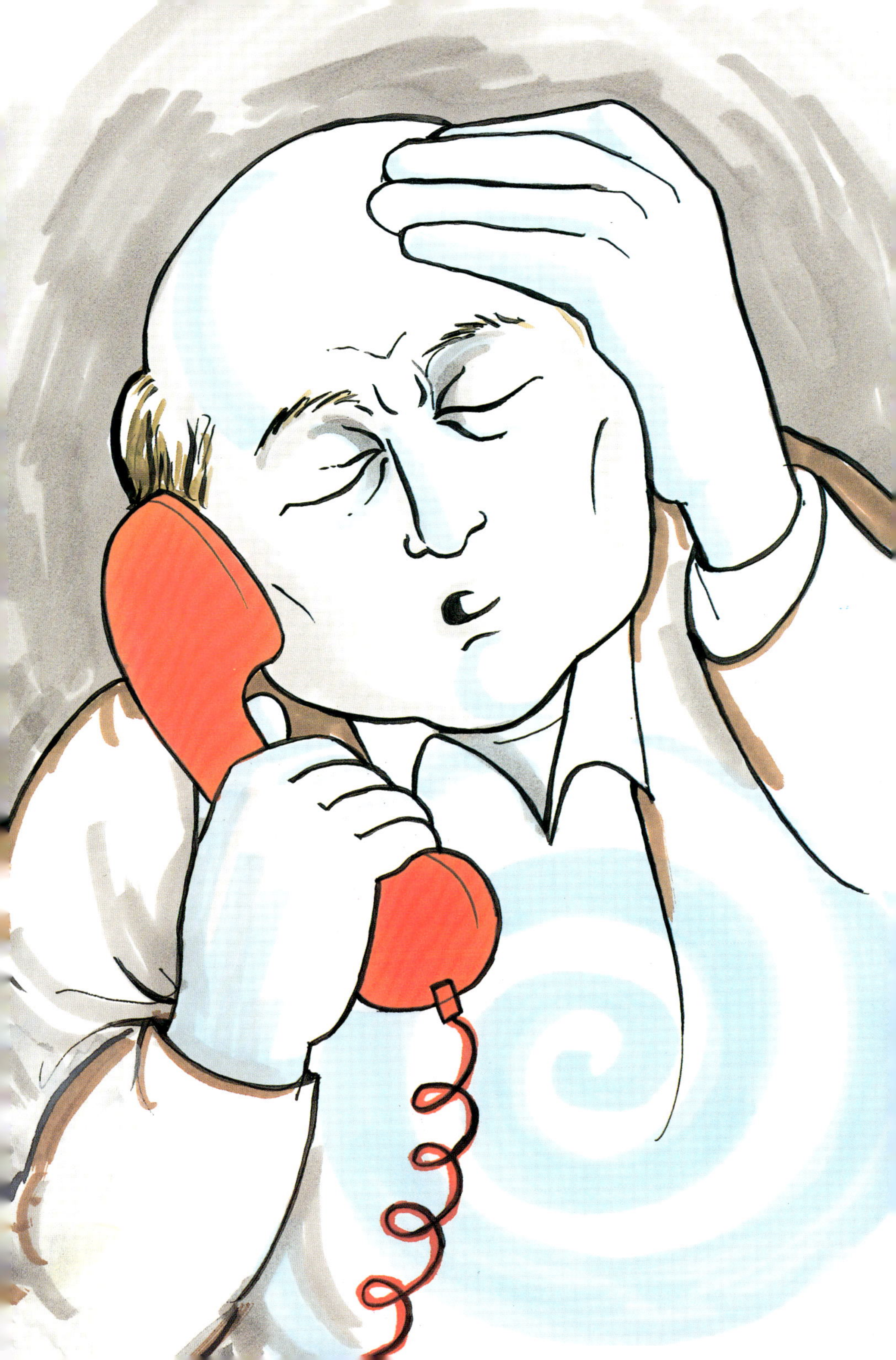

The ambulance came quickly and took Mum to hospital.

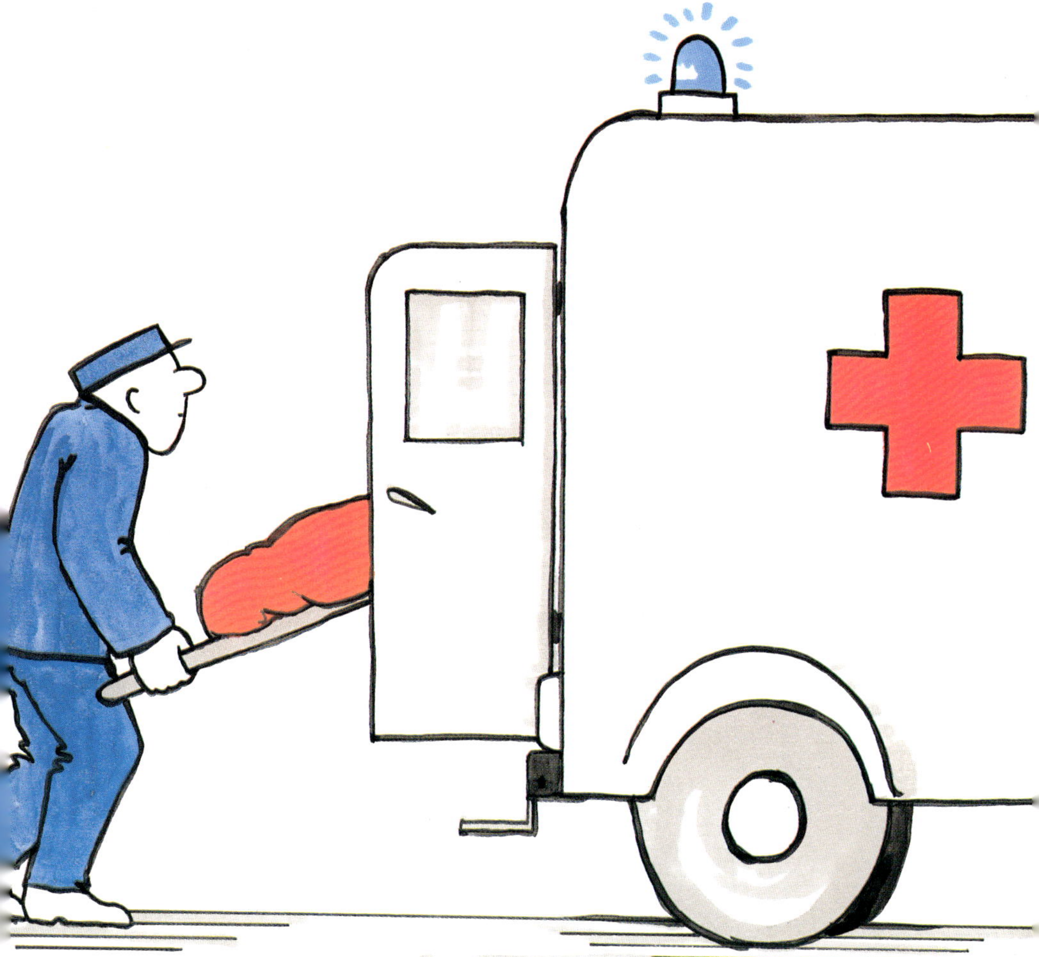

Dad, Stephen and Julie went to the hospital to see Mum.

Hospital

They bought some flowers to cheer her up.

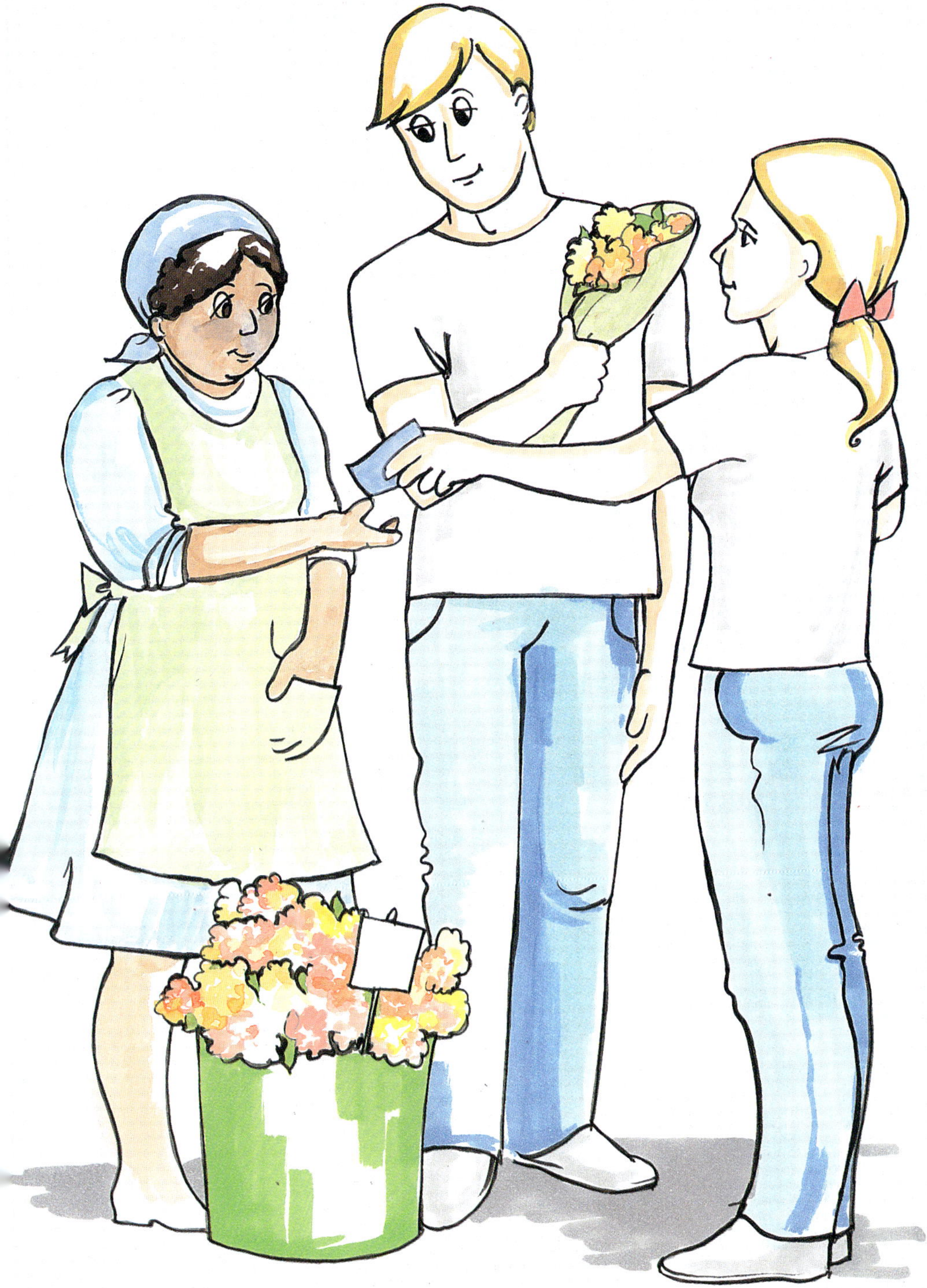

Mum was in bed because she was ill.
A nurse was looking after her.

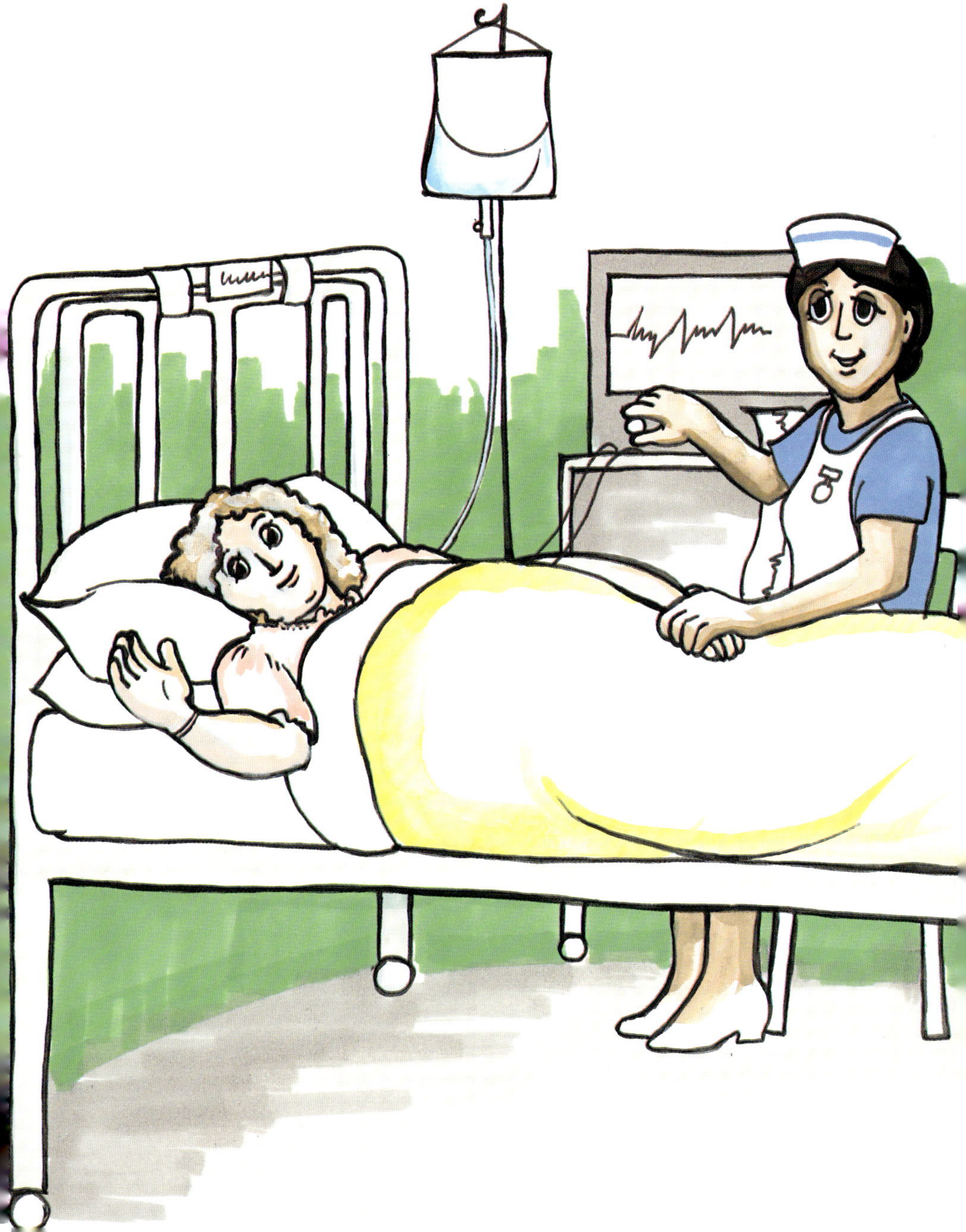

Mum was happy to see them.
They didn't know what to say.
Soon Mum got tired.
That was because she was ill.

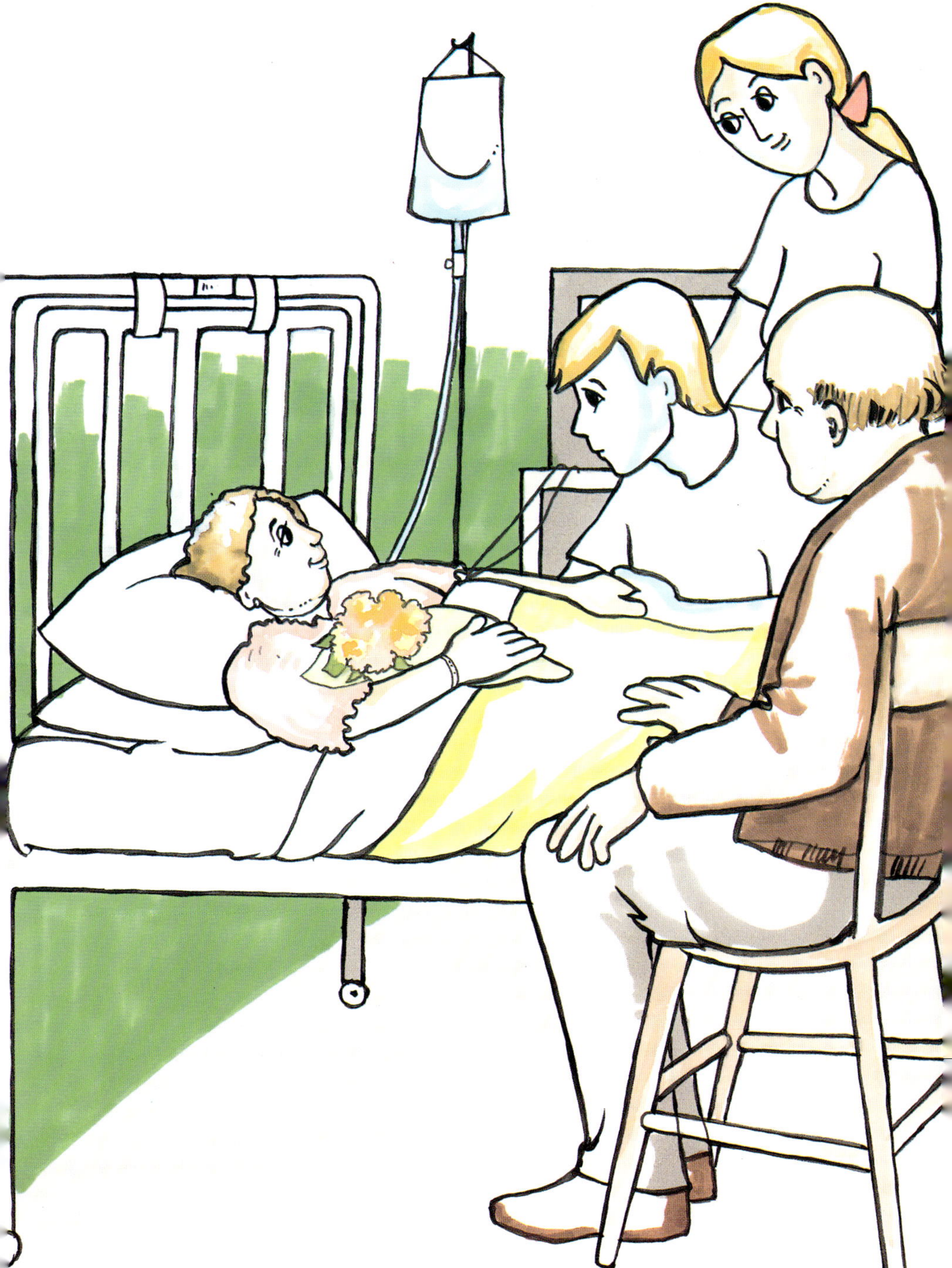

Dad said it was time to go.
They waved goodbye to Mum.

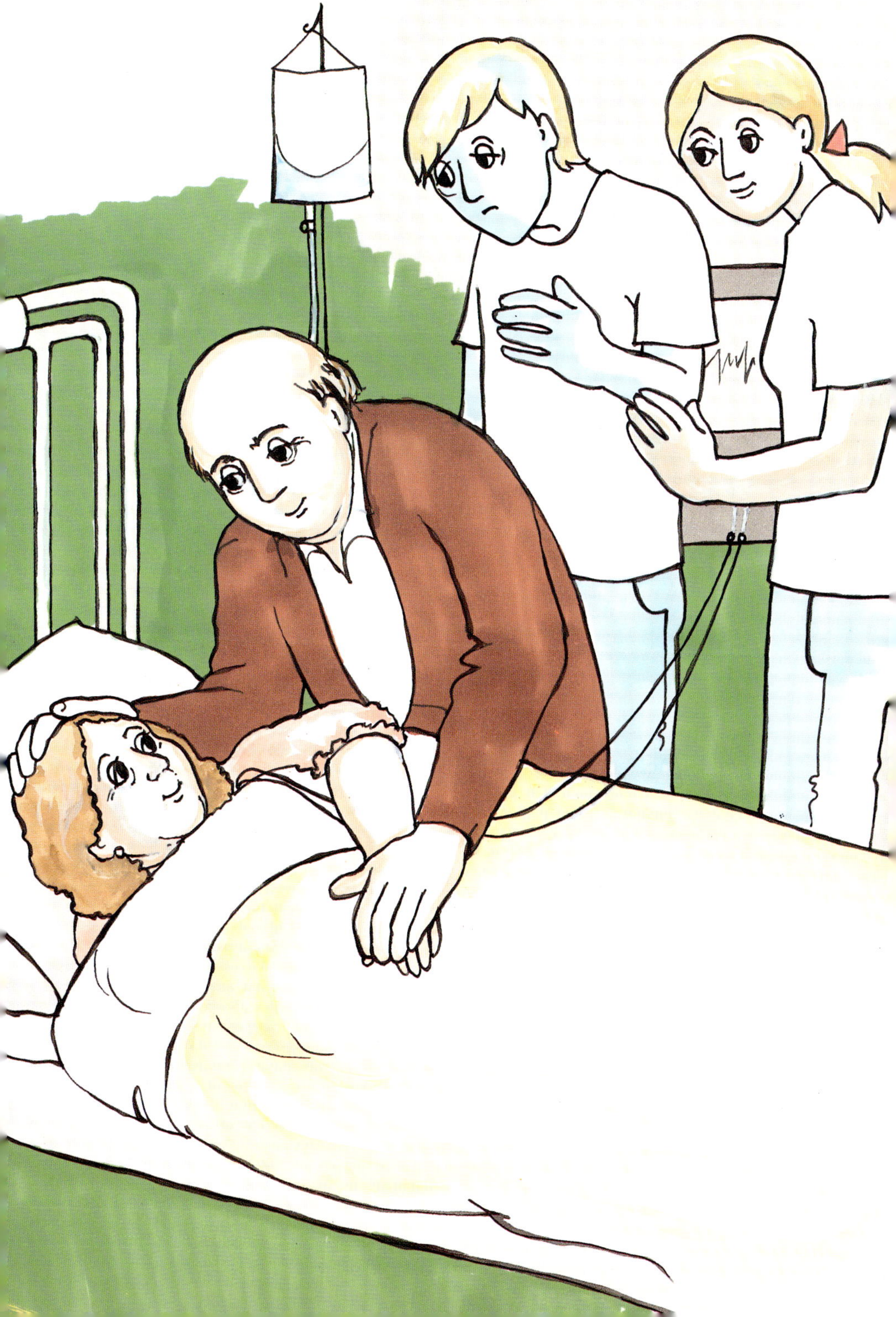

Dad said "Let's turn off the
television and talk about Mum."
Stephen didn't feel like talking.
He just wanted Mum to get
better.

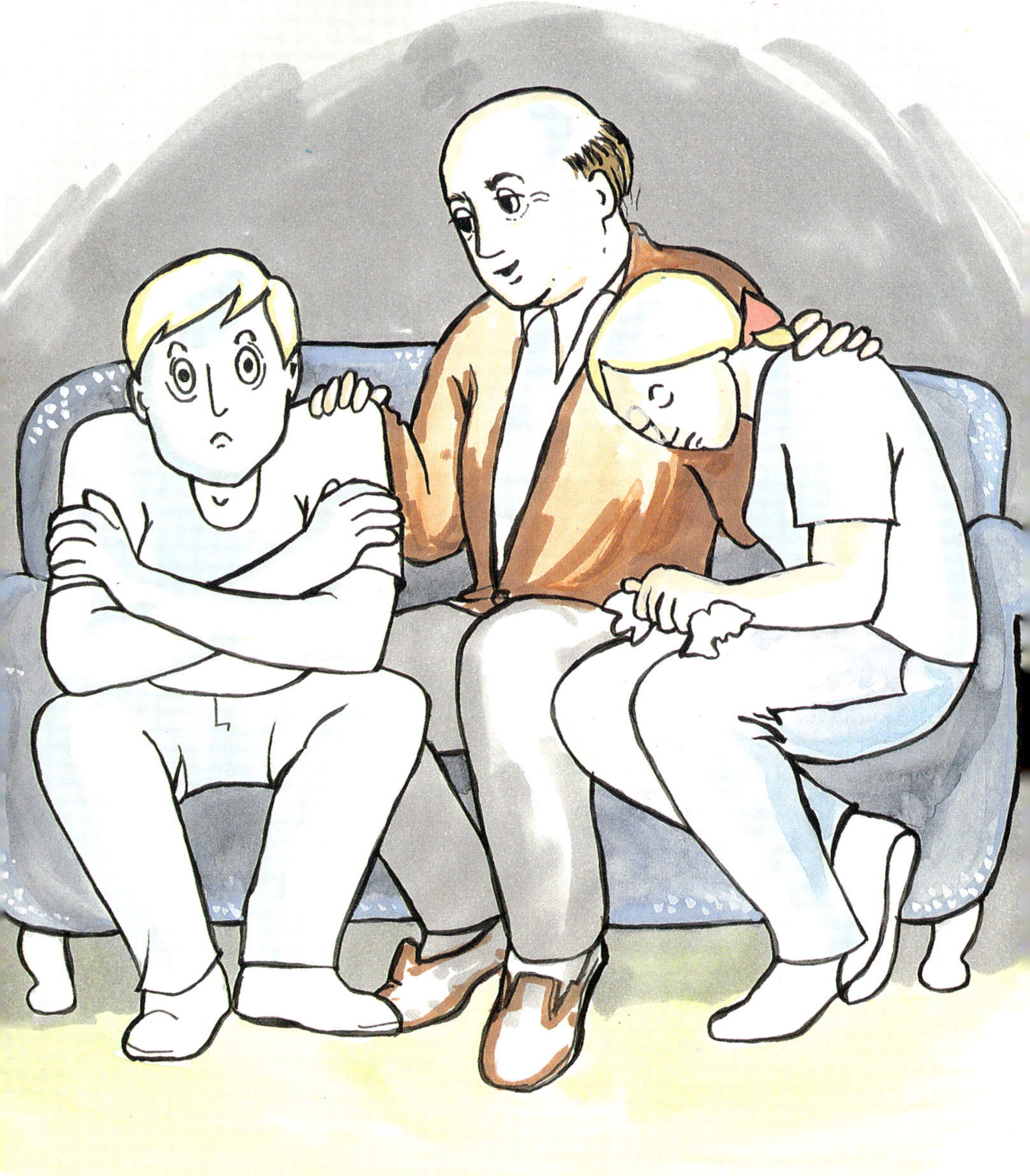

Mum was very ill.
She slept most of the time.
Stephen sat next to her bed.
He wanted to be with his Mum.
Sometimes his Mum woke up and looked at him.

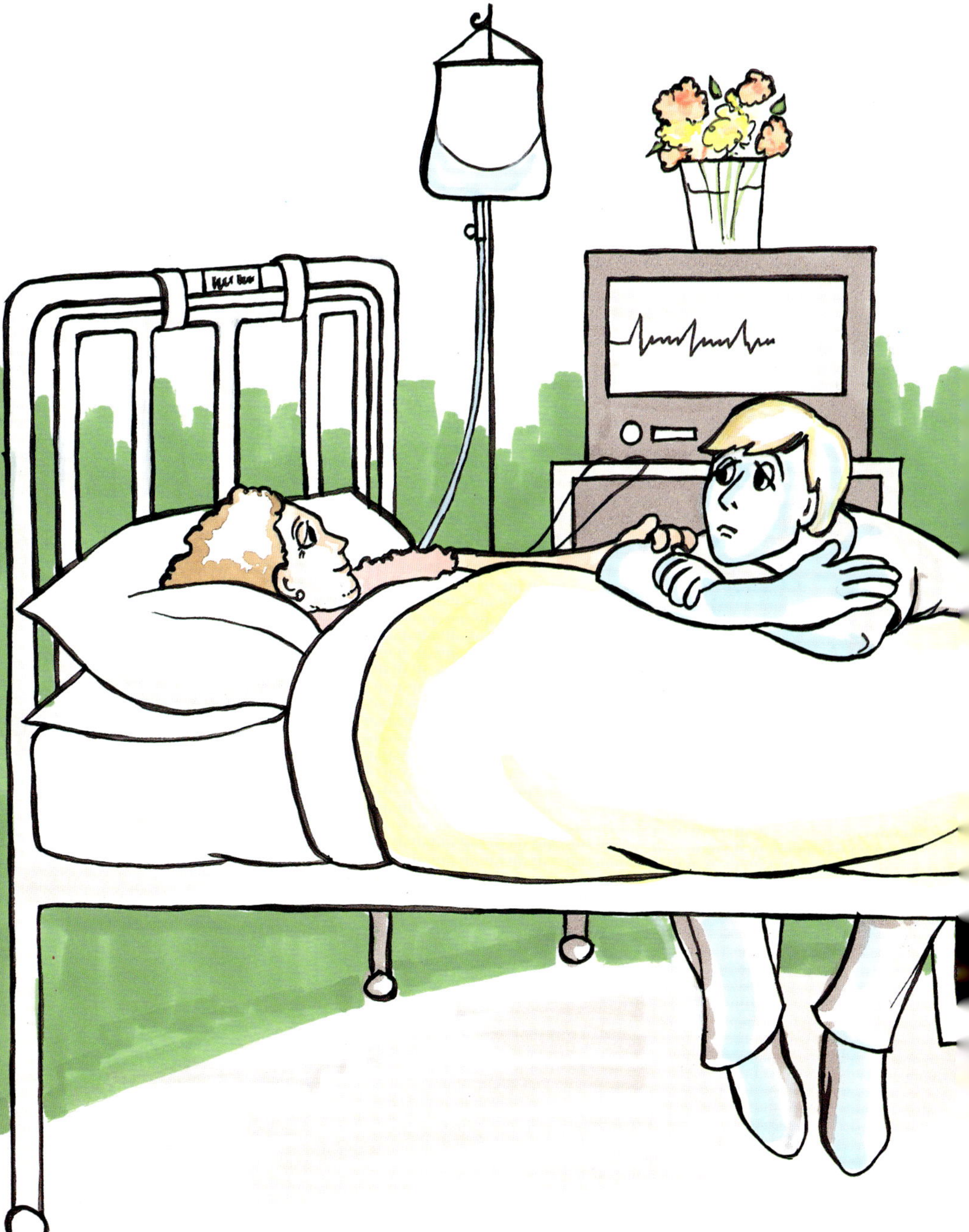

Stephen kissed his Mum.
He wanted to say goodbye.

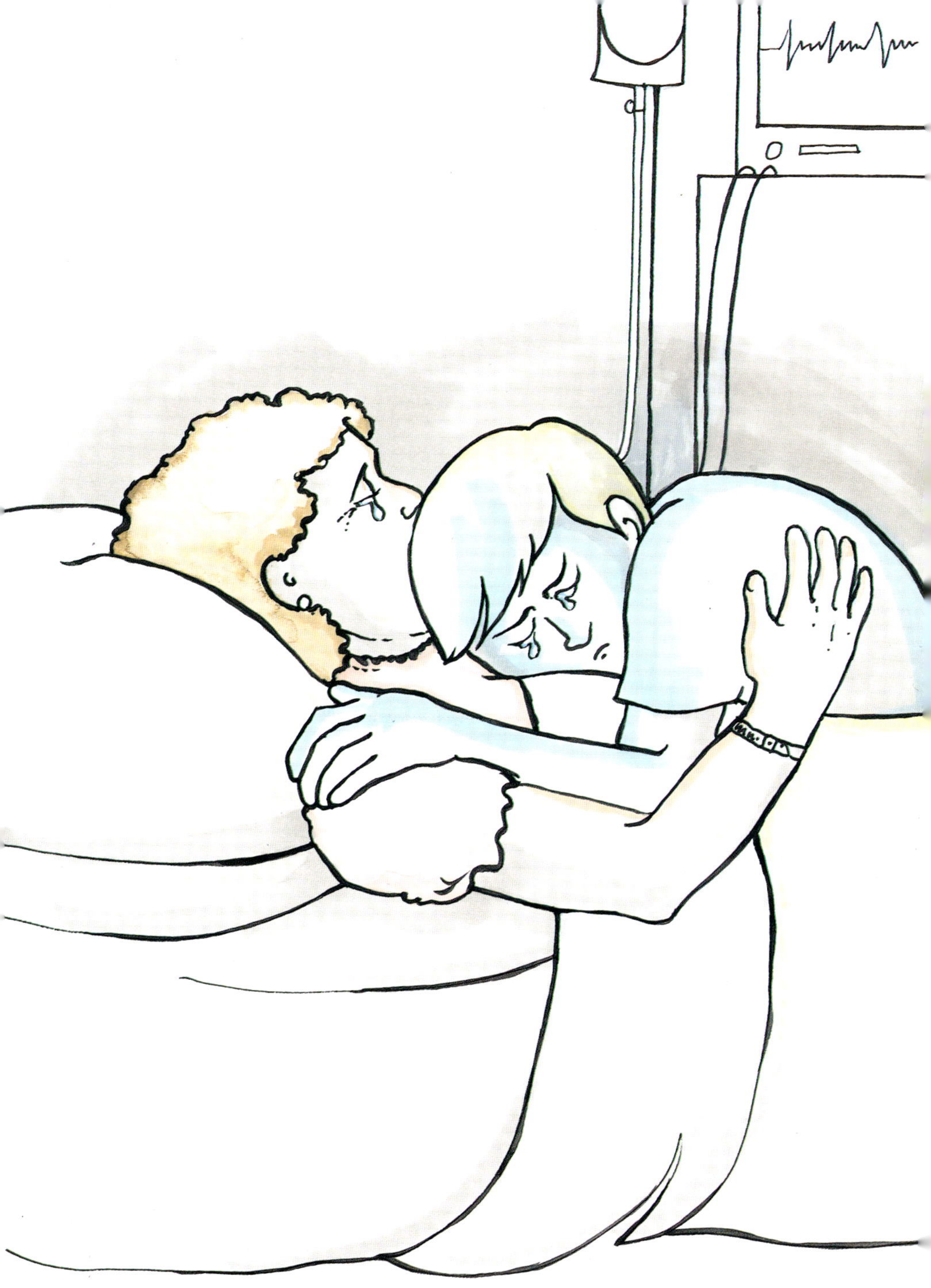

Dad said "I'm worried about Mum.
I don't think she'll get better."

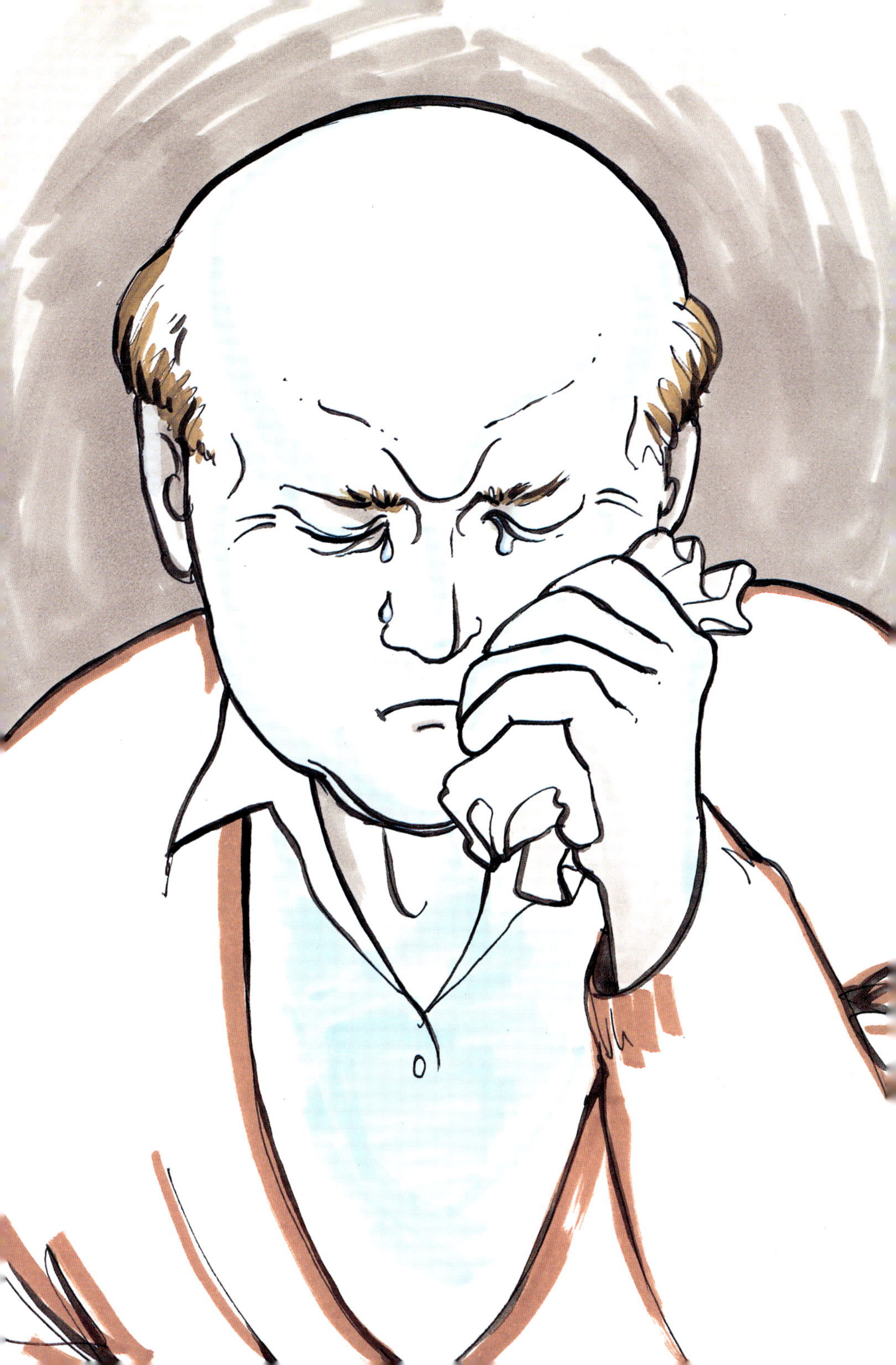

Later Stephen's Mum died.
She was not asleep.
She had stopped breathing.
She couldn't walk or talk or see anymore.

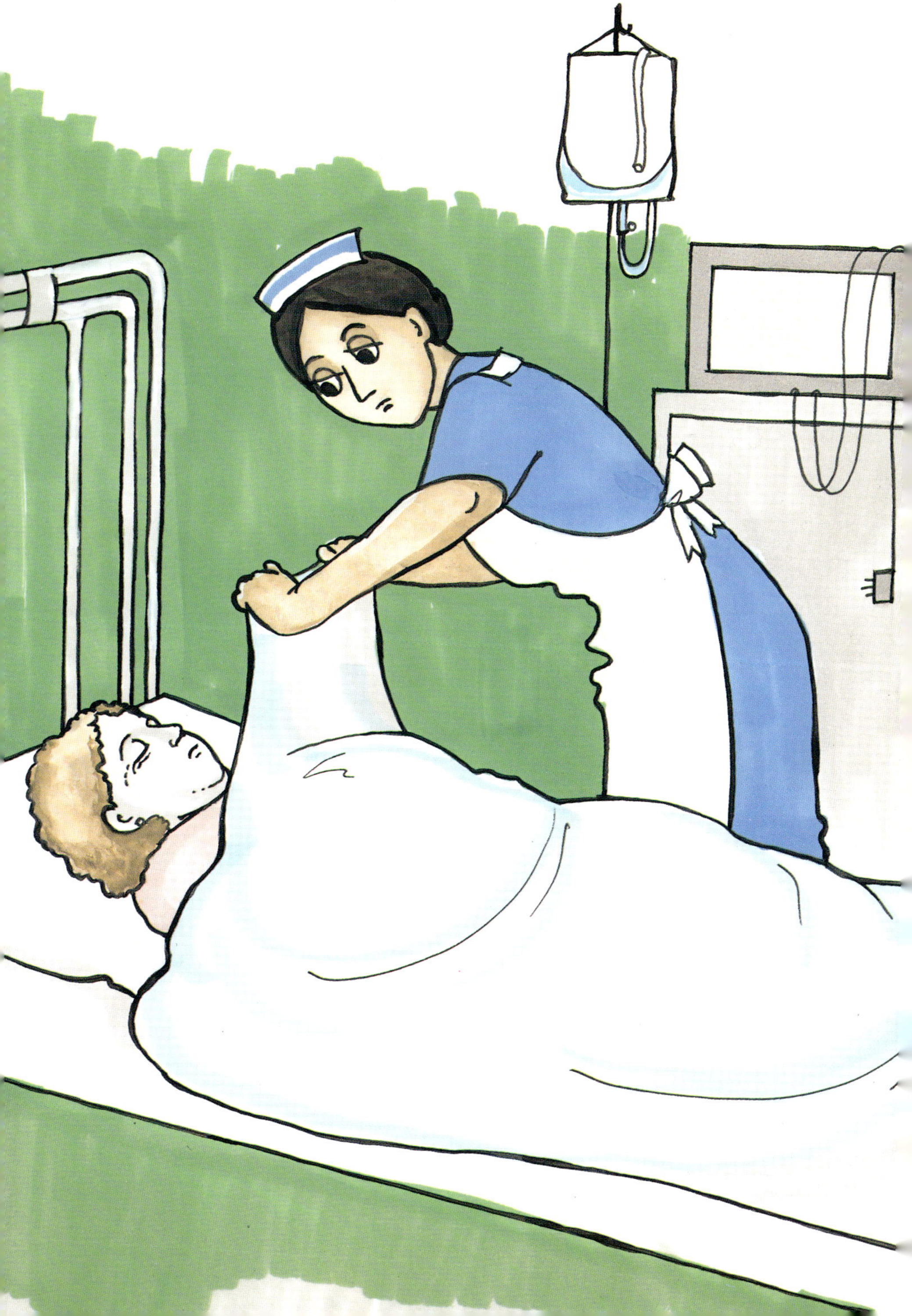

The nurse phoned Dad and told him that Mum had died.
Dad was very upset.

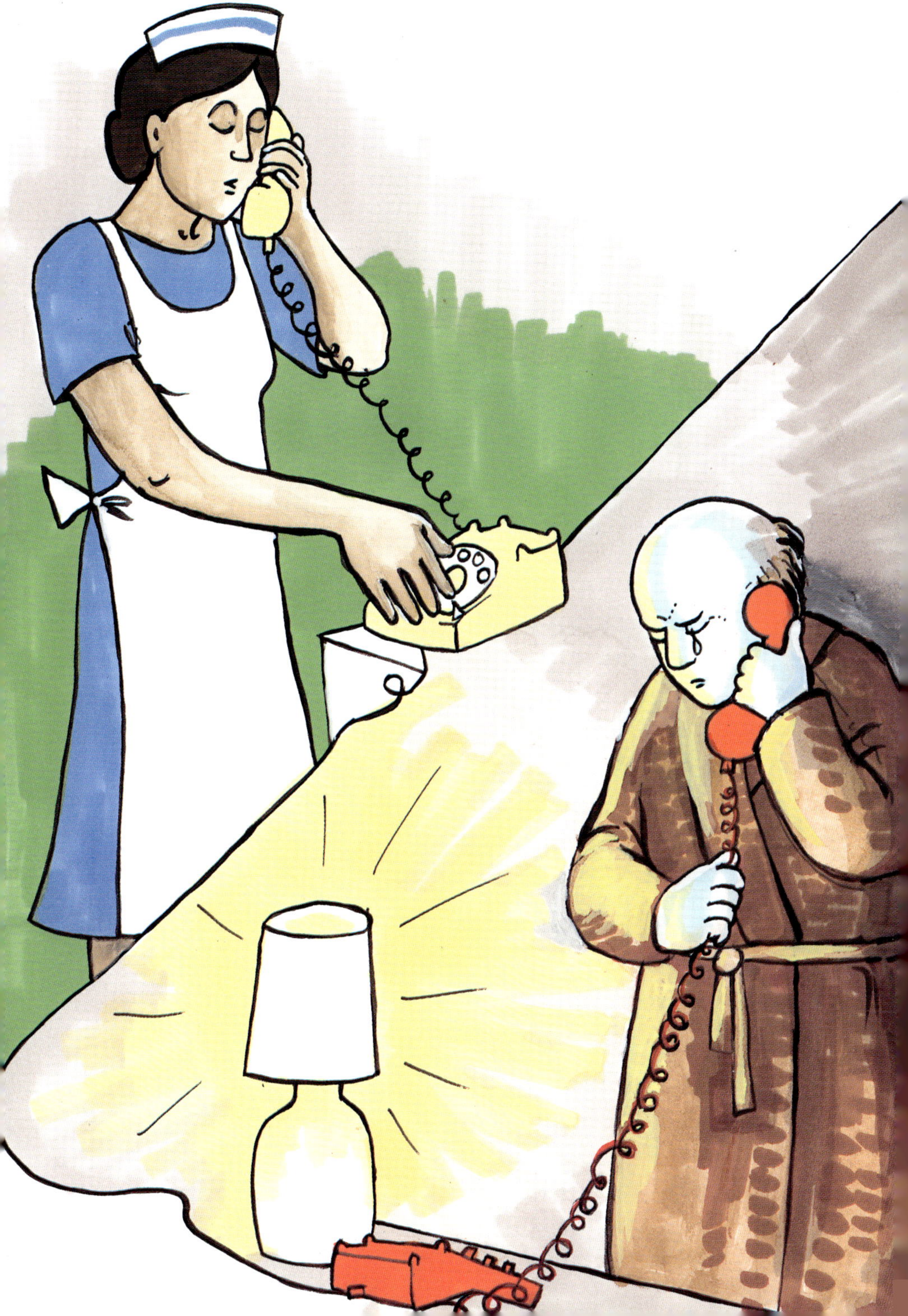

Dad woke Stephen up.
He had something very sad to tell him.
"Mum won't come home again. She died last night."

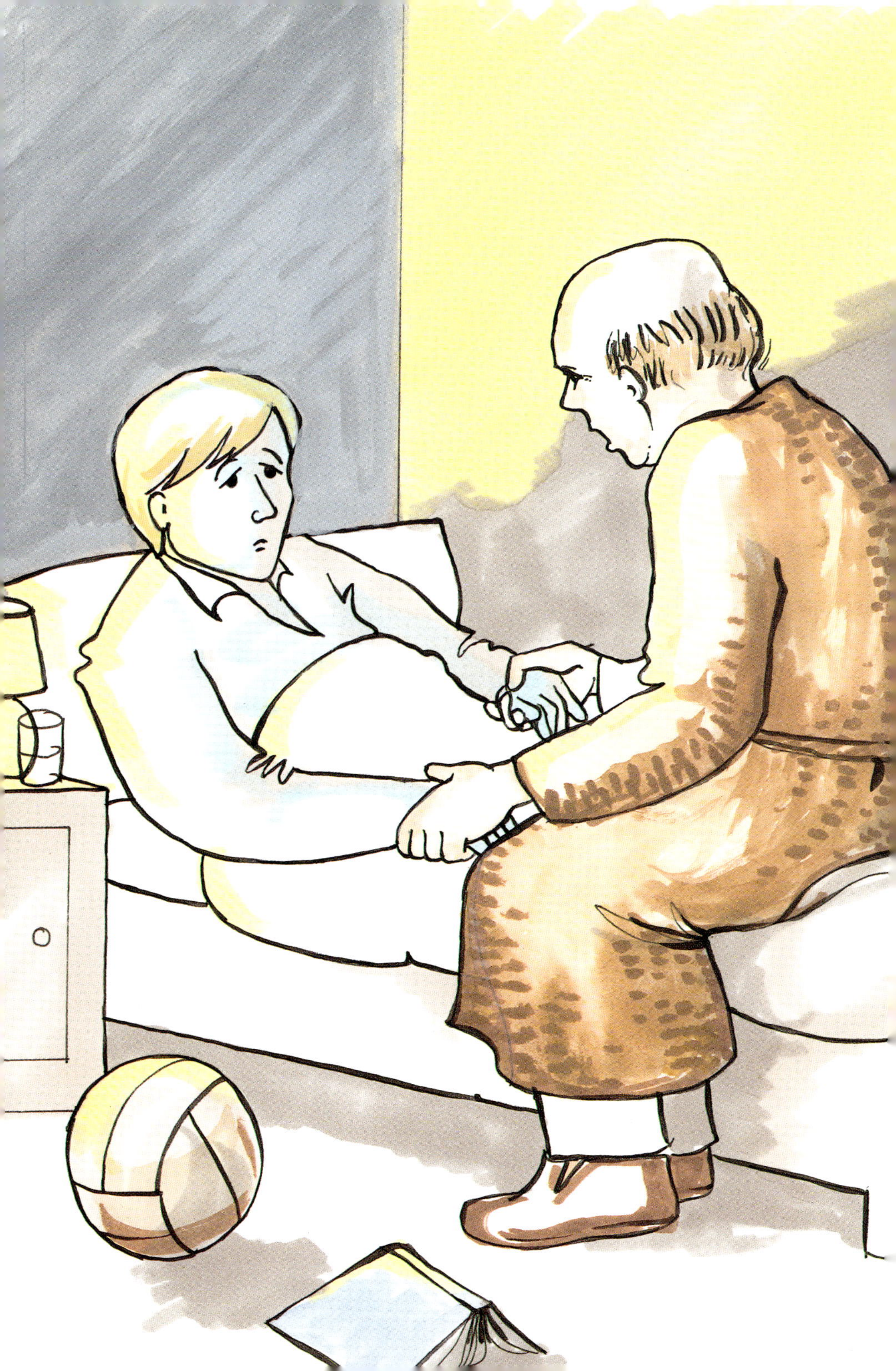

Stephen thought it was a mistake.
He wanted to go to the hospital to see Mum.
Dad wouldn't let him go and they had an argument.

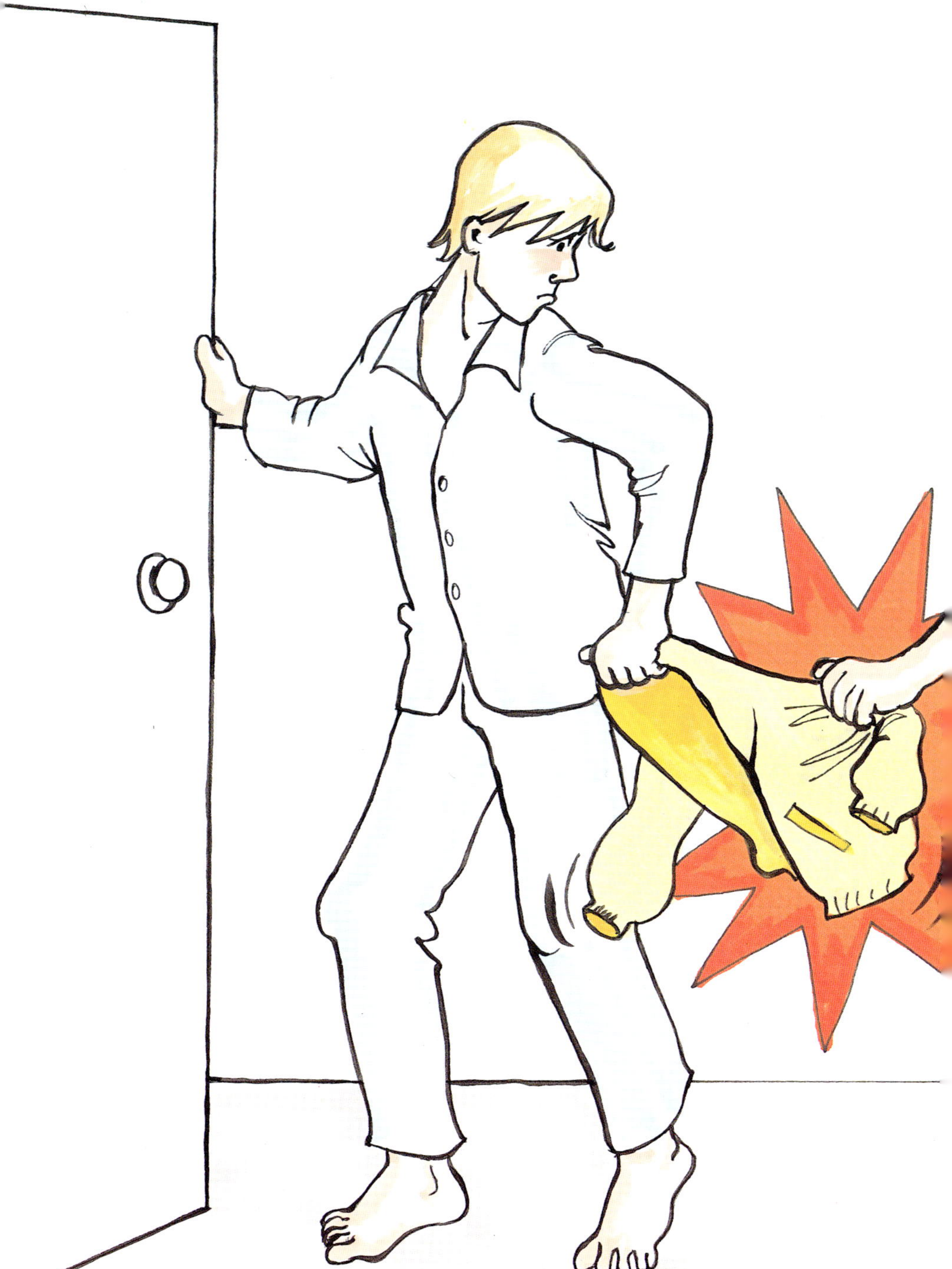

Stephen and Julie didn't
feel hungry.
They both felt upset.

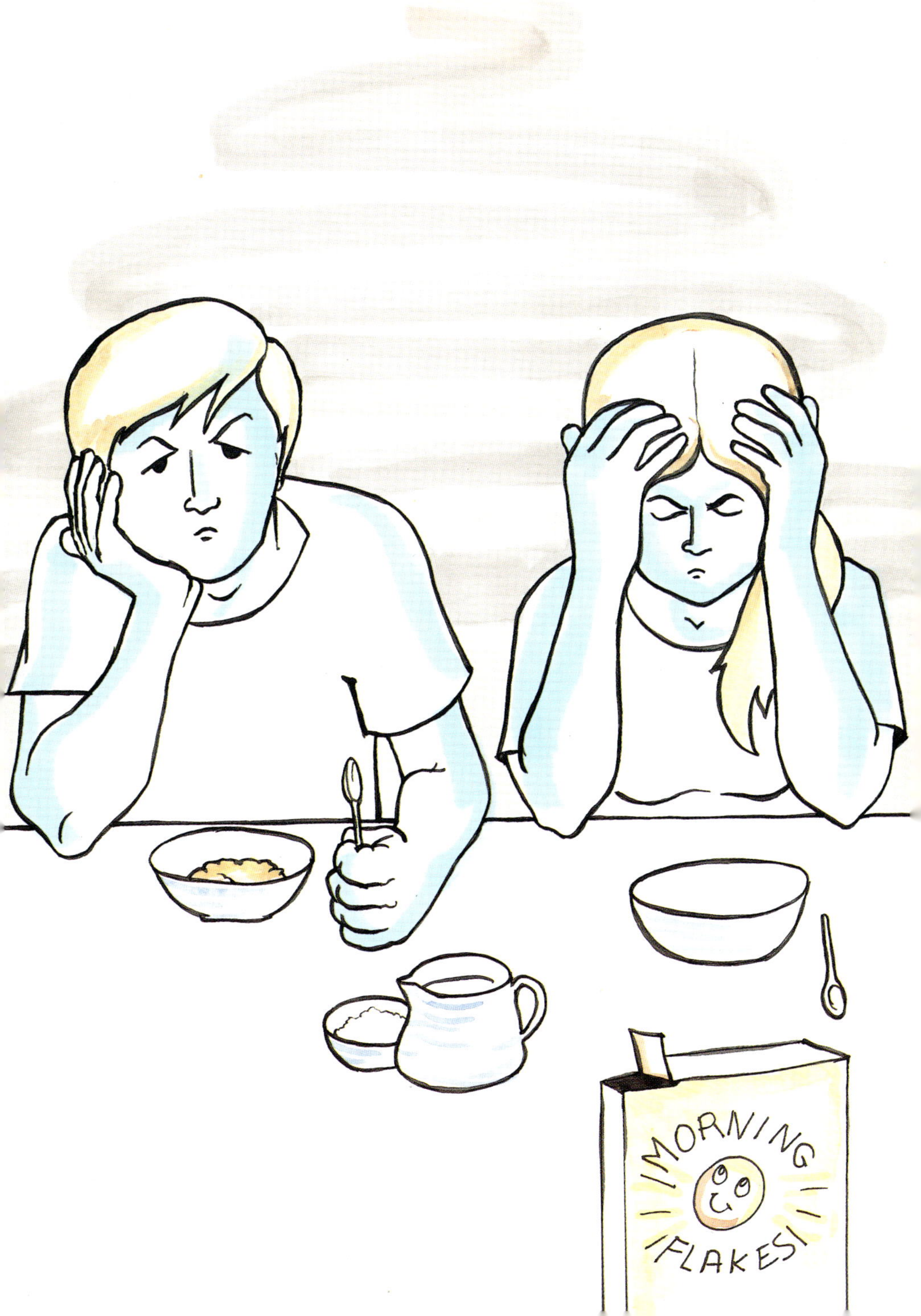
MORNING
FLAKES!

Stephen felt cross and muddled. He still didn't believe his Mum was dead.

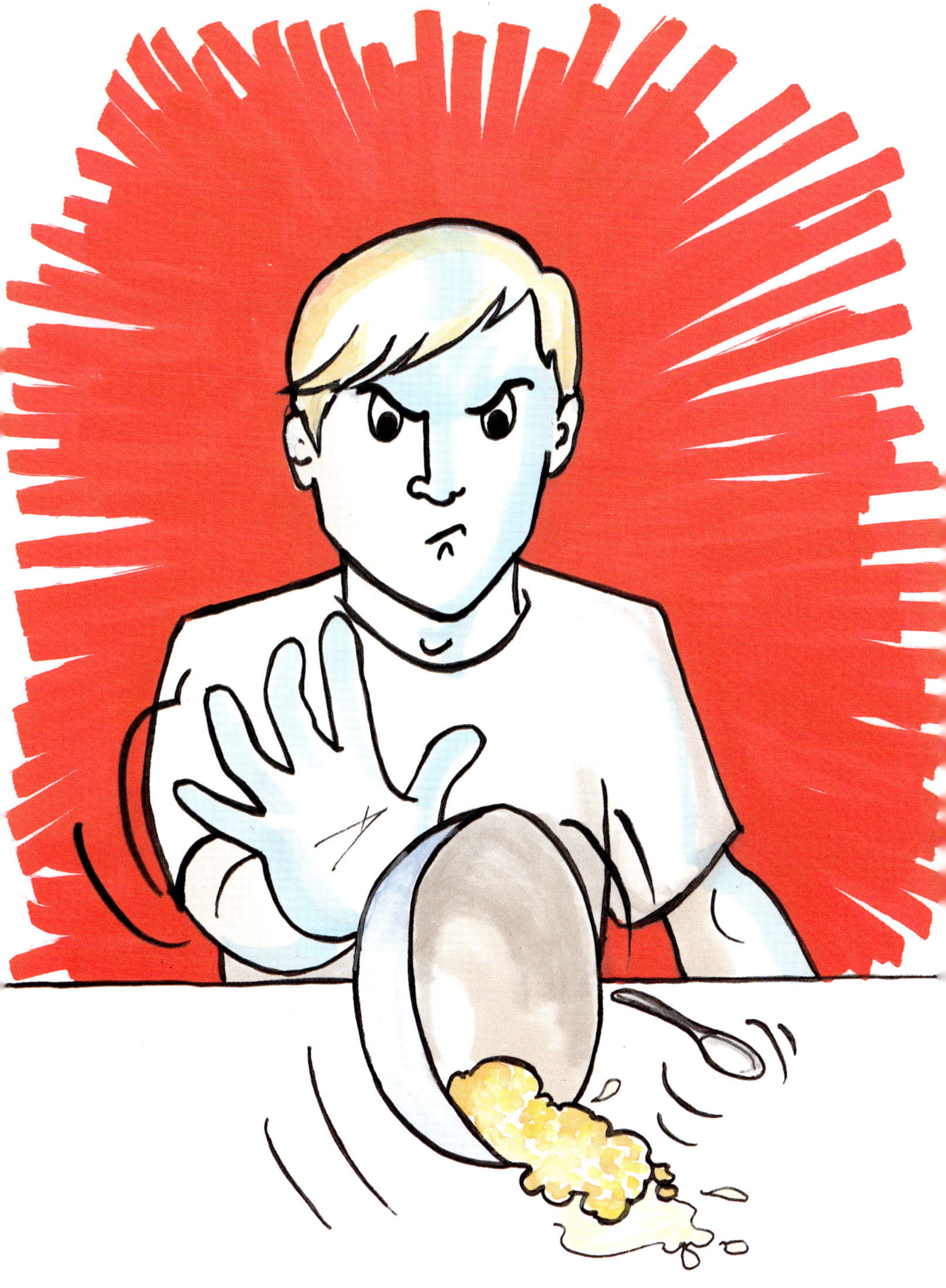

Dad knew why he was angry.
He told him again that Mum
was dead.
Stephen still didn't understand.

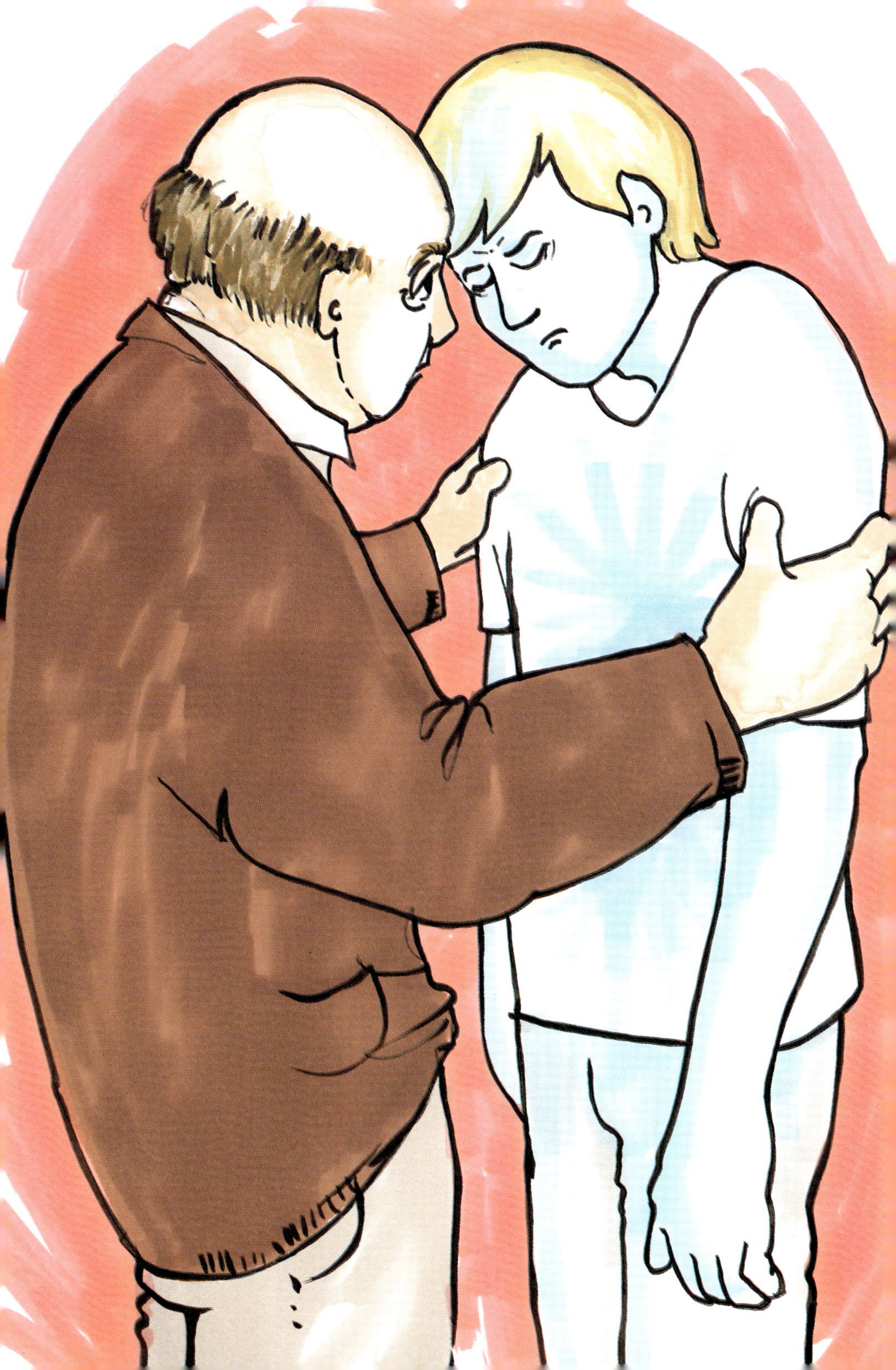

Next day they went to see Mum.
Her body was in a coffin.
Then Stephen understood that she was dead

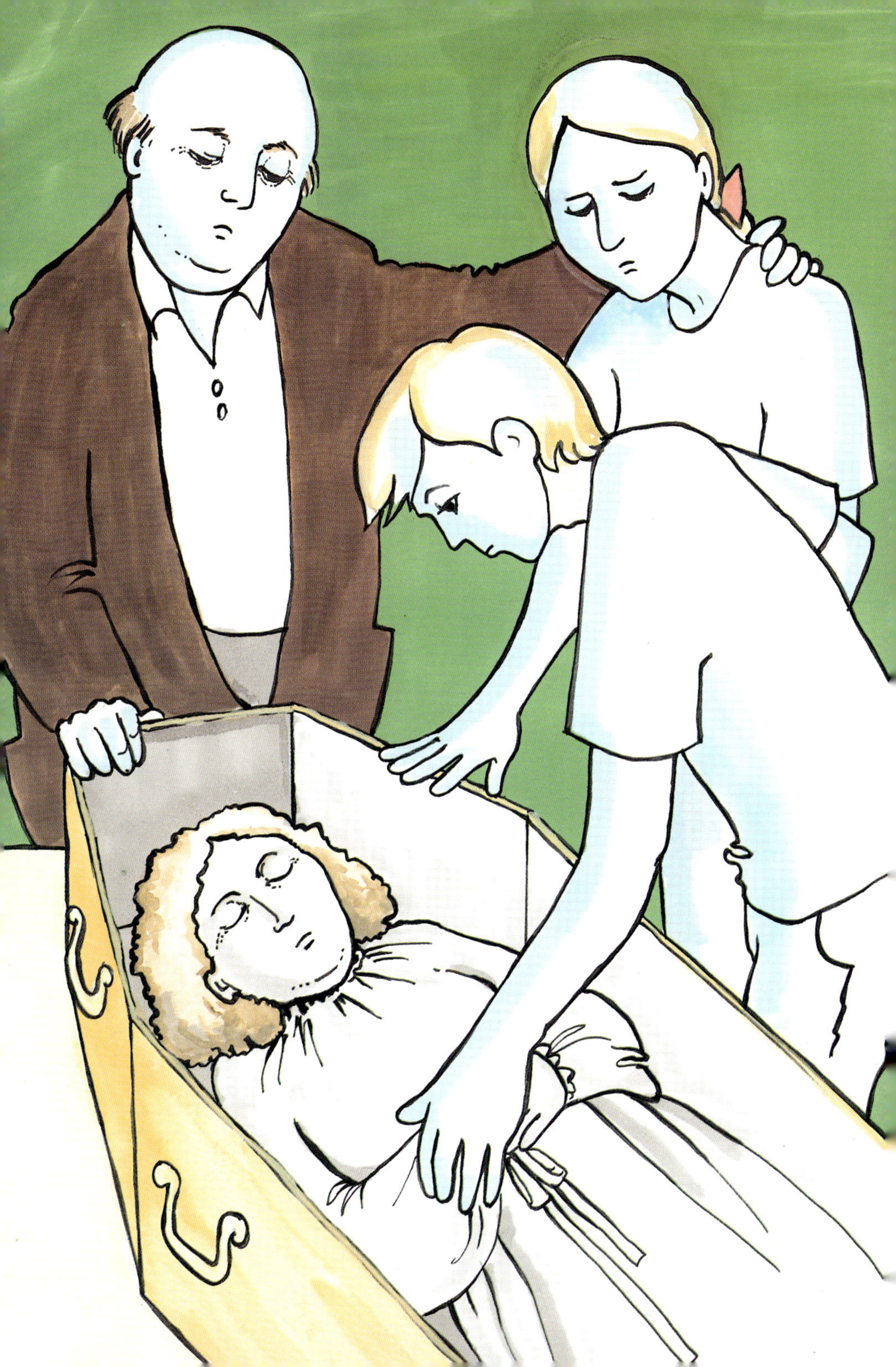

Mum's coffin was driven to
the cemetery.
Stephen, Julie and their Dad came
in a different car.
Mum's friends came to
say goodbye.

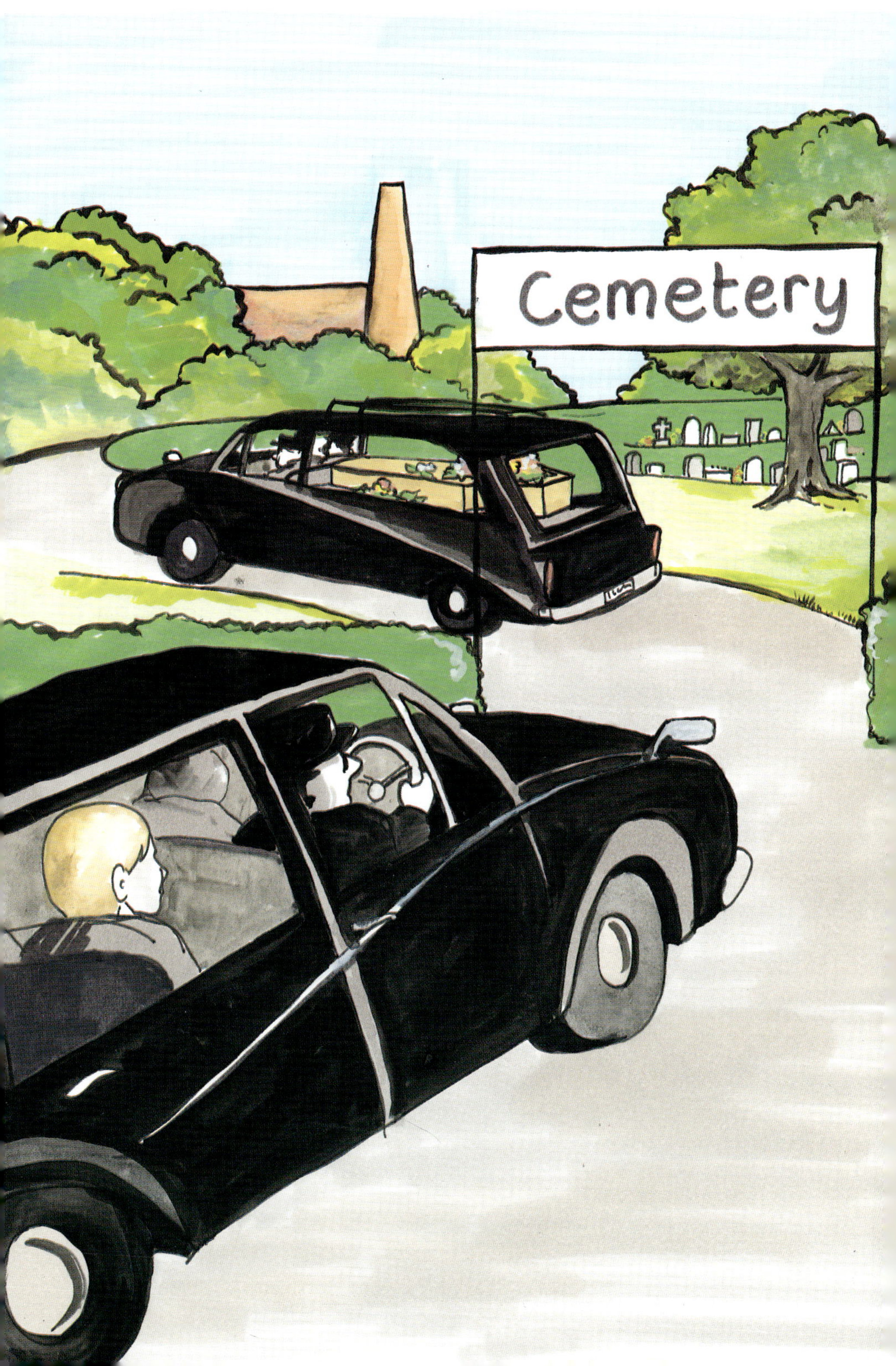
Cemetery

Everyone said goodbye to Mum.
Stephen wondered why Mum had died.
Was Mum with God?

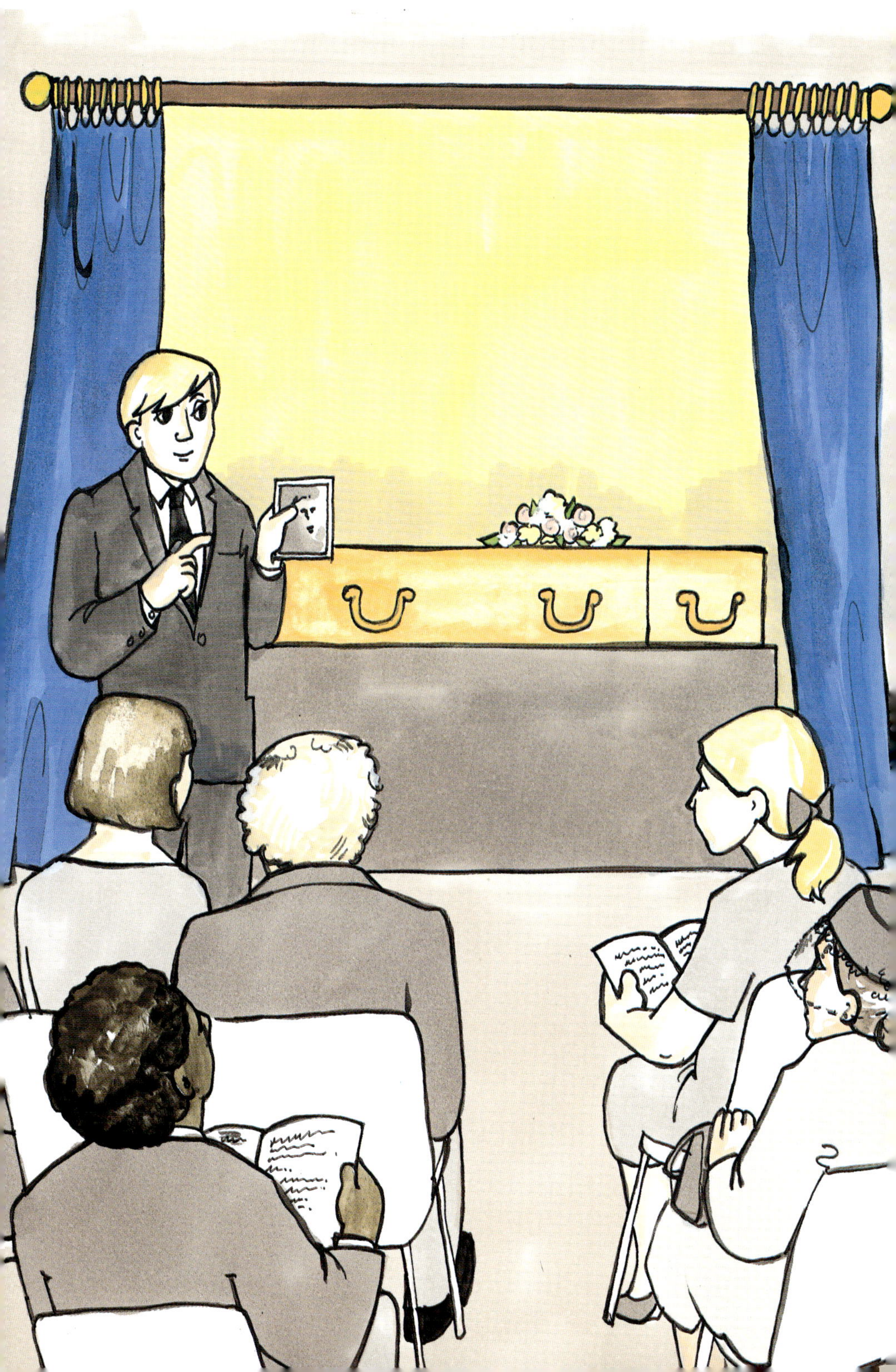

Mum's body was put in a hole in the ground.
There were lots of graves in the cemetery.
Some had headstones with people's names on.

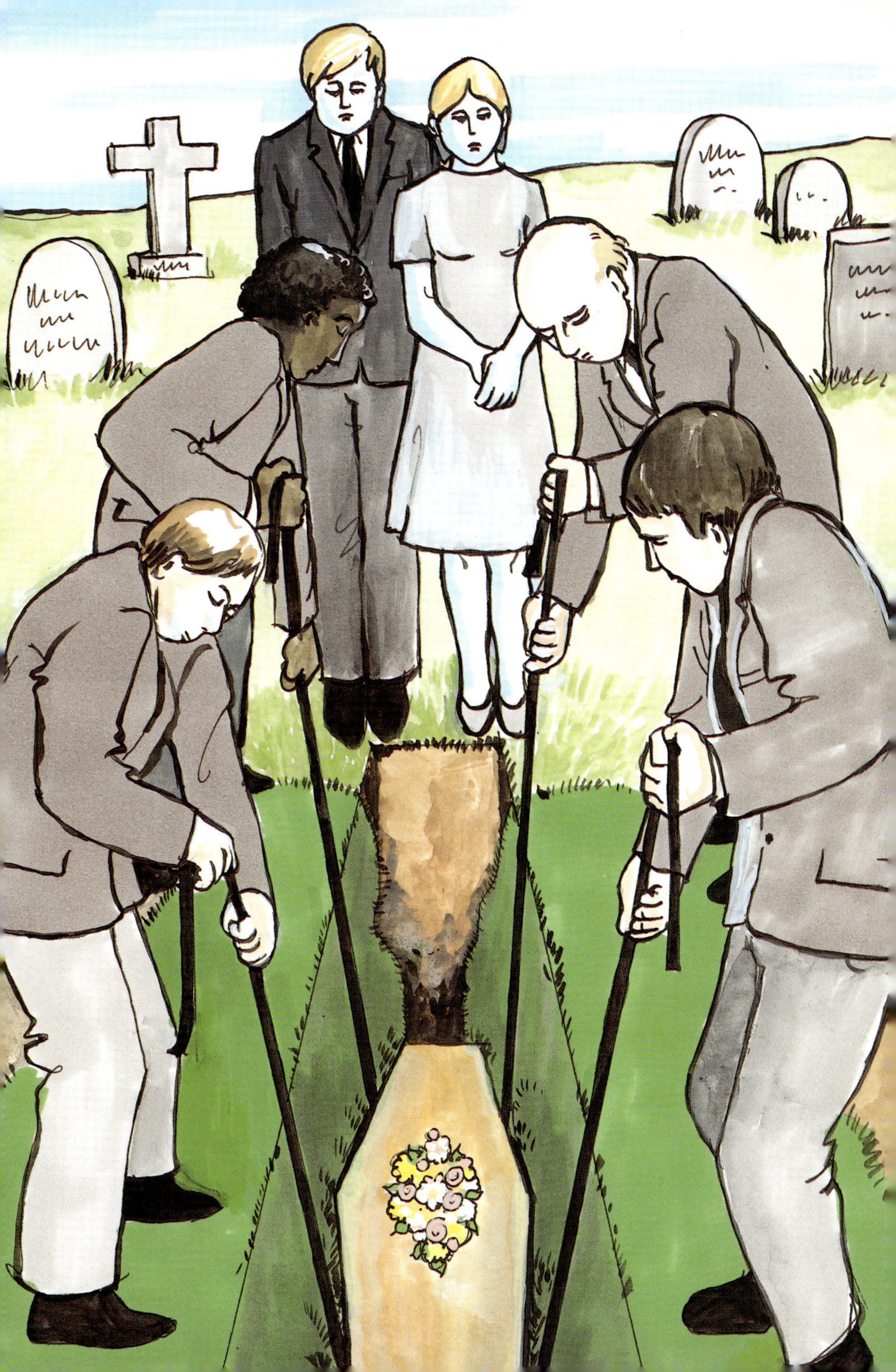

Sometimes Stephen felt lonely.
He didn't want to play with
his friends.
They didn't know what to say.
They were glad it was not their
Mum who had died.

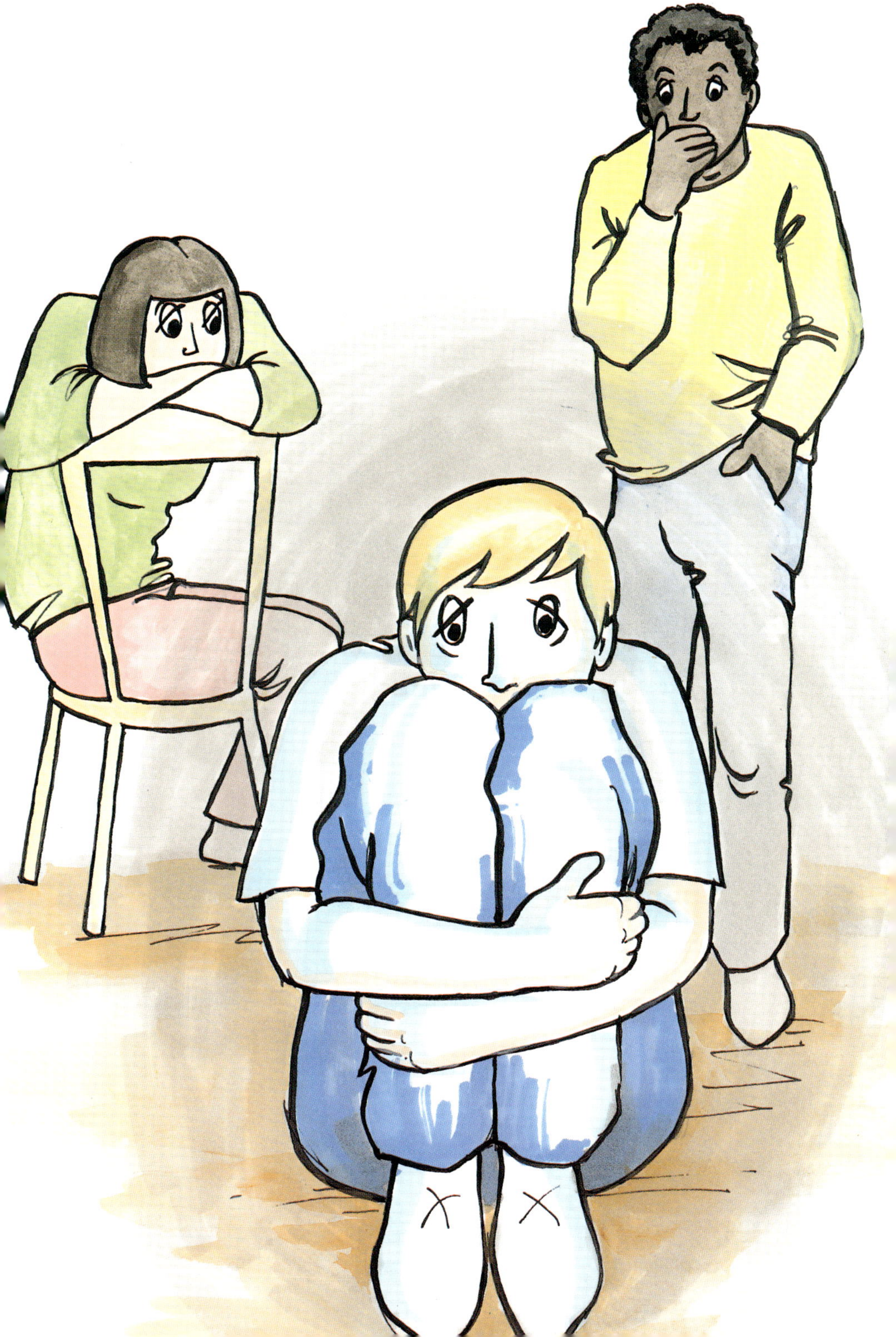

Stephen and Julie planted a rose bush with Mum's name on it.

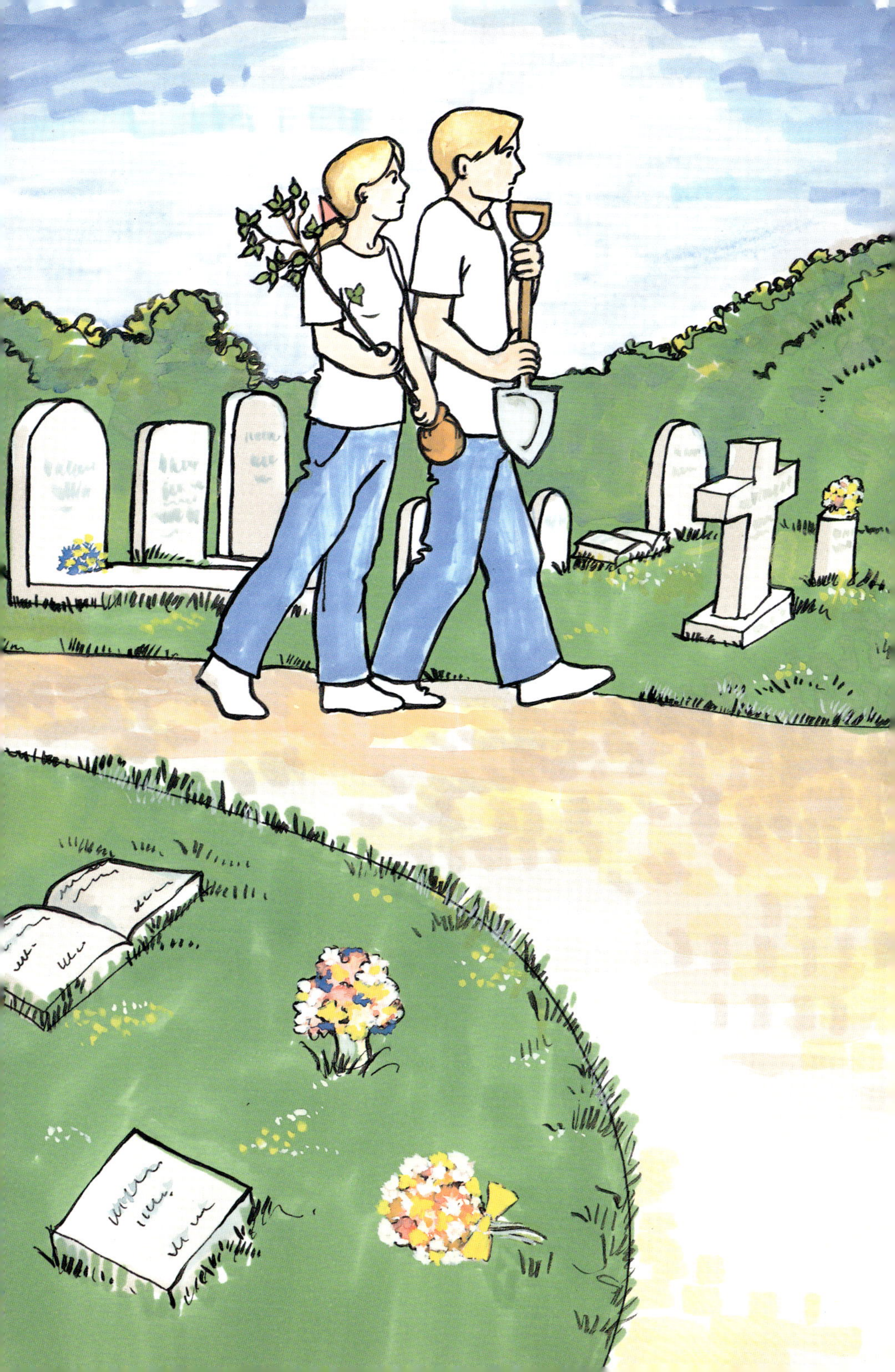

Dad gave Stephen and Julie a photograph of Mum to keep. Stephen felt sad all over again. Dad told Stephen that Mum wanted him to have her camera. That made him feel happy.

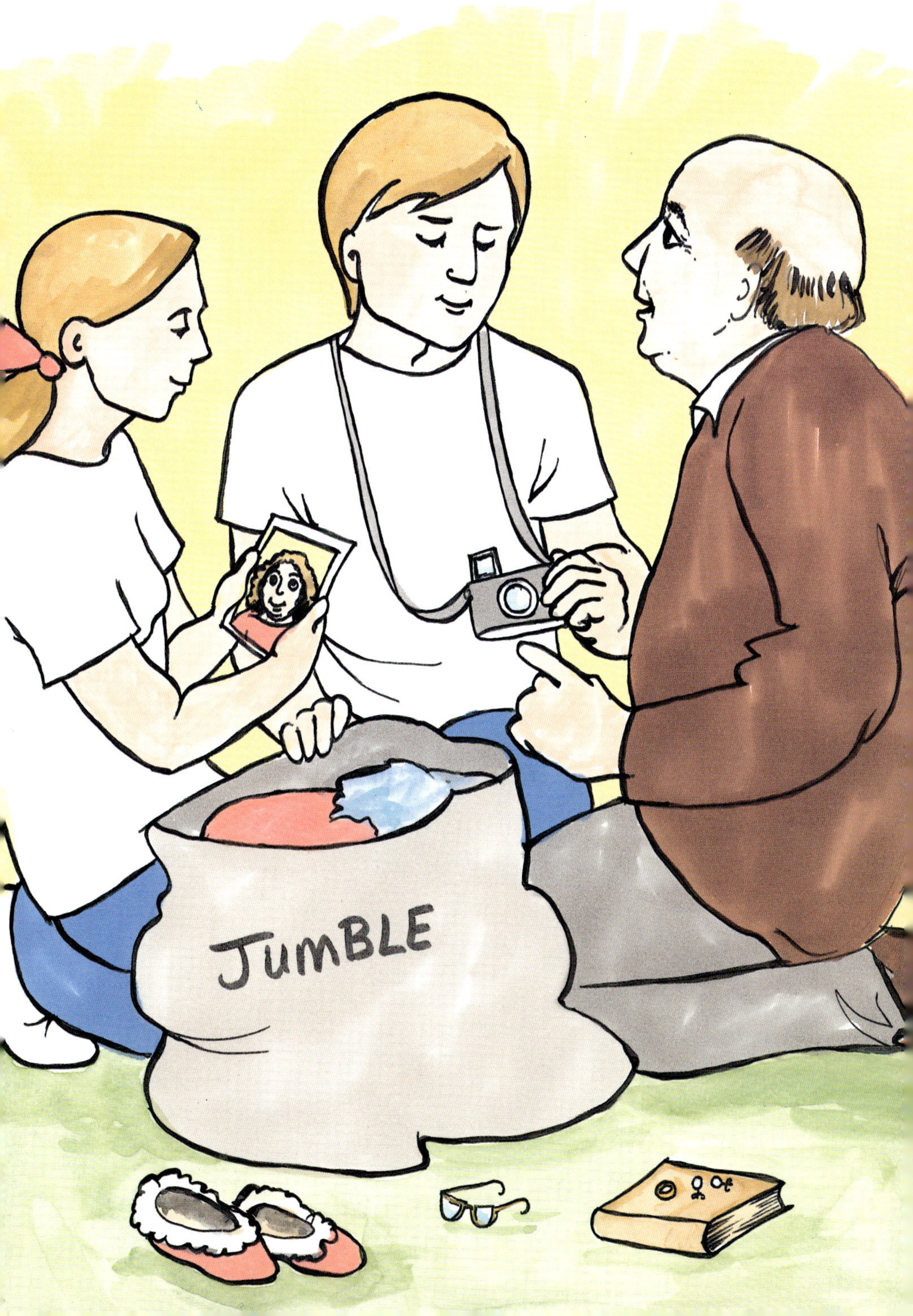
JUMBLE

They were still a family.
They had good times together, and
they often talked about Mum.

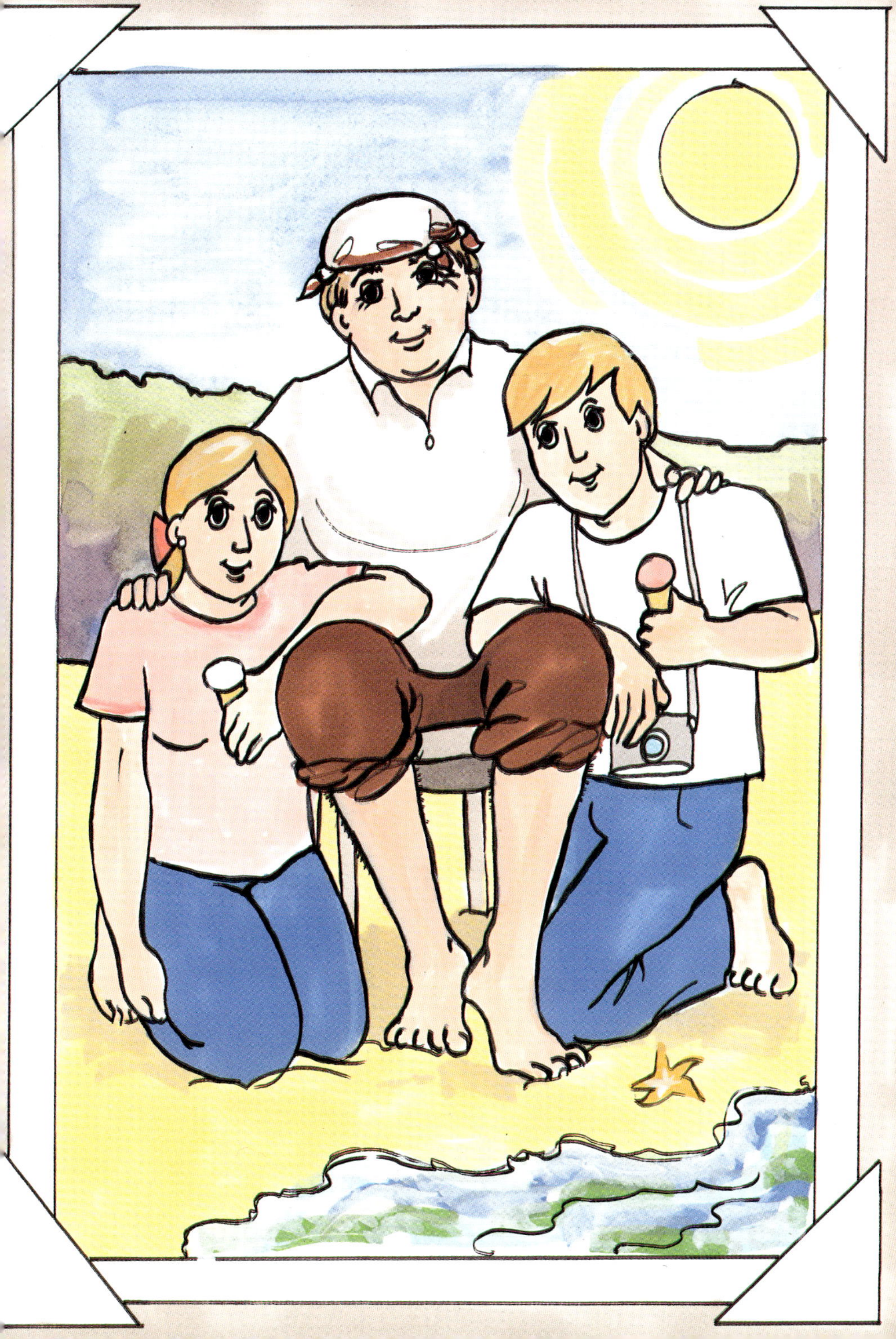